BIG.
FAT.
MISTAKE.

And Other Stories We Write Together

ONCE UPON A PANCAKE
Making Reading and Writing Fun

BIG. FAT. MISTAKE.

And Other Stories We Write Together

STARTED BY RICK BENGER

Collins

An imprint of HarperCollins*Publishers*Ltd

WRITTEN BY

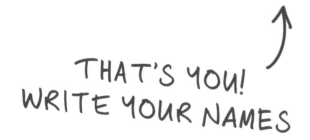

THAT'S YOU!
WRITE YOUR NAMES

STARTED BY Rick Benger

LEAD ILLUSTRATION BY Maddie Egremont

EDITED BY Karin Fisher-Golton

COVER DESIGN BY Zeena Baybayan

HOW THIS BOOK WORKS

STEP ONE

Grab a pen, pick any story inside, and come up with what happens next. Write a little or a lot. Make it silly, scary, poetic, action-packed, magical. Go wherever your imagination takes you.

STEP TWO

Pass the pen. It's someone else's turn to write.

STEP THREE

Repeat! Keep taking turns. Giggle, make mistakes, help each other. When you finish, you'll have a unique story that only you and your friends could have created.

HAVE FUN!
RICK

Leon can hardly believe it. He's really here, in the stadium, for the World Cup semifinal, with five of his best friends from his soccer team. They've even made special shirts to spell out the name of their favorite player, Bobby Brooks.

They get a mountain of drinks and snacks, then find their seats. In all their excitement they forget to sit in the right order—of course they should be spelling B-R-O-O-K-S. Instead they're spelling K-R-O-B-O-S.

STORY #1

Big. Fat. Mistake.

STORY #1

...CONTINUED

WHAT DOES
KROBOS DO?

STORY #1

Nobody had seen Old Man Jenkins in twenty years, and Mo was determined to find out why.

Every night, Mo looked out from his bedroom window, with binoculars, across the lake at the house where Old Man Jenkins lived. The only sign that Old Man Jenkins was still alive was the mellow candlelight dancing on the curtains in an upstairs window. And sometimes, when it was an especially calm night, Mo heard a bone-tingling sound carry over the lake. It sounded like ....

....

....

....

....

STORY #2

STORY #2

"Can you keep a secret?" asked Julia.

I thought about it for a moment. The real answer was no. Secrets wriggle and bubble inside me until I burst and out they come.

"To be honest, probably not," I said, feeling pretty good about being honest.

"I'll tell you anyway," she said. "Last night I ....

....

....

....

....

....

....

....

....

....

....

....

....

....

....

....

....

STORY #3

DID THE SECRET
STAY SECRET?

Rosa had done nothing wrong.

Well, that's not exactly true. The instructions inside her new toy kit, the Robo-Master-Maker Special Edition, *did* say never to make anything during a thunderstorm. And Rosa had to admit that it was a little thundery and a tiny bit stormy when she completed her latest masterpiece, which she named

....

....

....

....

....

SOUNDS BAD.
WHAT DID ROSA'S
MASTERPIECE DO?

....

....

....

....

....

....

....

....

STORY #4

KEEP GOING . . .

...CONTINUED

WHOA. IS
THAT ROSA'S
MASTERPIECE
OR ANOTHER
ROBOT?

STORY #4

STORY #4

Dear Diary,

I saw the future in my dreams again. That's 3 times now. They can't all be coincidences, can they? I'm freaking out!!

First, there was that dream where the floor in our classroom was lava and it was a gazillion degrees and everyone's books were on fire. And then the next day there was an actual fire in the school cafeteria, and we all got evacuated.

Then there was the dream about

And then the next day

And this morning I dreamed

Should I tell anyone? What if my dreams are making these things happen?

STORY #5

May 16th

Dear Diary,

It's my first time on an airplane. I'm in my seat, excited to finally know what takeoff feels like, looking out the window at the baggage workers who look like little Lego people on little Lego carts.

"Hi there," says somebody from the aisle seat. I turn around to say hello, but only manage a weird, gurgling "Hrrghh."

It's . . . . On my plane. Talking to me. For real.

. . . .

. . . .

SOUNDS LIKE SOMEONE FAMOUS. WHO?

. . . .

. . . .

. . . .

. . . .

. . . .

. . . .

. . . .

. . . .

. . . .

STORY #6

STORY #6

It was official: Alana was a queen—the new queen of a place called Hippotopia, according to a boy with lilac-colored skin who appeared, bowed before her, and said, "Alana, my queen! At last I've found you. You must come with me. We don't have much time, because ....

....

....

....

....

....

....

....

....

....

....

....

....

STORY #7

STORY #7

To get to the school bus stop, Emi had to walk past the house with the vicious, beastly, terrifying hellhound.

At first, she dreaded walking alone. But over time she learned how to sneak by, quiet as the moon, light as the clouds. She didn't realize it yet, but she was becoming a ninja.

FINISH THE COMIC!

WHAT DID EMI USE HER NINJA SKILLS FOR?

STORY #8

W e returned from winter break to find a statue of ....
....

....

in front of our school. No one knew how it got there, ← ADD A NAME

least of all me and my friend ....

But our principal, Mrs. Fong, called us into her office and said, "I know you

two are responsible. If you don't confess now, you'll be expelled."

    "We didn't do it!" we pleaded in chorus.

    "Lying will only make matters worse," said Mrs. Fong.   UH-OH

....

....

....

....

....

....

....

....

....

....

....   KEEP

   GOING...

STORY #9

DRAW THE
STATUE →

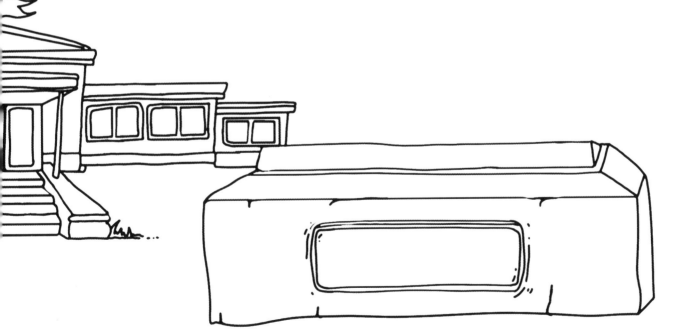

STORY #9

...CONTINUED

HOW DID THE
STATUE GET
THERE?

STORY #9

DID THEY PROVE
THEY WERE
INNOCENT?

Every seven years, at the first dawn of spring, a giant tree in Lotusville blooms with edible purple flowers that last for exactly one week.

They call it the .... tree because the flowers taste delicious—so delicious, in fact, that for the whole week all the grown-ups in Lotusville simply hang around the tree smiling, chatting, and munching away. They don't hustle or bustle. They don't frown or fret. Life is good, and worries can wait.

It's a story as old as Lotusville that any child who eats a special flower will turn into a ghost. But James is skeptical. He's never seen a ghost-child. "What if that's just a story told to stop us children from having fun?" he wonders. Maybe he should try a flower. Just one.

STORY #10

STORY #10

At last, I have my own bedroom.

My parents told me I can decorate it any way I like, with one condition:

WHAT'S THE CATCH?

DECORATE
THE ROOM

The whole country hasn't had hypernet for five days.

Everyone's losing it. Mom and Dad don't know what to do without their BusyBots. My sister is carrying on like she's the only one who has to suffer, boo-hoo, and all she's really missing out on is that stupid series about old English people.

I have a real reason for losing it—I need to figure out what a Zaggzok is. And who Professor Vincent is. Otherwise my friend Jason will rot in jail on Mars.

Okay, okay, you're thinking, who said anything about Mars? Cool your jetpack! I'm getting to that, like right now.

Jason's parents are mega-rich. They have their own rocket and go on vacation to this fancy resort on Mars every year. It's called .... Jason said maybe he can take me one day.

Anyway, this was the last message I got from Jason before the hypernet went down . . .

WHAT'S A
ZAGGZOK?

KEEP GOING...

...CONTINUED

"Are you Professor Vincent?" I whispered.

"Maybe. Who's asking?"

WHO IS
PROFESSOR
VINCENT?

IS JASON
RESCUED?

STORY #12

It was a normal Wednesday for Rayvan. School was okay, karate practice was awesome, and while walking home through the park she daydreamed about pizza. Karate always made her want pizza.

So she was walking, triple-pepperoni on her mind, when she saw a stick on the ground next to the giant willow tree and thought, "Huh, a magic wand." Then she thought, "Huh, I'm going crazy."

But wand or stick, it called to her. It looked like

....

....

....

....

....

....

....

....

....

....

....

....

STORY #13

STORY #13

Can I tell you something embarrassing?

I hated it when Grandma moved in with us. I know that's not nice. But I only hated it because it meant I had to share a room with my brother, Liam, and he's definitely not nice.

It's turning out great, though. Grandma is super fun. She is an awesome dancer, and she ....

....

Grandma is also a bit of a daredevil. She comes up with wild schemes and convinces me and Liam to play along. ....

....

SUCH AS?

....

....

....

....

....

....

....

....

....

....

....

STORY #14

Now of course Emory knew that throwing a disc in class would mean instant detention. But the disc in question was a brand new birthday gift from his friend Tyler. It would be rude not to seem excited. And Tyler was only like six feet away. And Mrs. O'Callaghan wasn't looking.

Emory's throw was perfect, sort of, almost. But Tyler ....

....

....

....

....

....

STORY #15

In the town of Little Creek, all music was gone.

When Aisha strummed her guitar, there was no thrum. When Simon struck his bass drum, it didn't go *bom*. And when Benjamin blew into his hands to play the national anthem in farts, the farts were silent.

No music, not a single note nor beat, was heard in all of Little Creek for weeks and weeks—until Aisha woke up in the night to the most enchanting, most beautiful guitar playing she'd ever heard. It was coming from outside. She put on a jacket, tiptoed past her parents' bedroom, and

WHO WAS PLAYING?

WHAT HAD HAPPENED
TO THE MUSIC?

FILL IN THE COMIC!

Rohan fell asleep, faceplanted on his desk, and dropped his pen on the floor. Again. Everyone laughed. Again.

It wasn't his fault that he kept falling asleep in class. He had to fight crime at night. And lately, there had been a whole lot of crime.

He bent down to pick up his pen and noticed something on the underside of his desk.

Meet me at locker E307 at lunch time. Come alone. B.G.

STORY #17

WHO IS "B.G."?

KEEP GOING . . .   STORY #17

A BIG BOX FOR A BIG FINISH!

"I dare you," she says.

I know, I know. I shouldn't feel like I have to do stuff just because someone dares me. But I can't help it. Especially because it's Gabriela who's doing the daring.

WHAT'S THE DARE?

GABRIELA

STORY #18

Dante thought that Mr. Van der Snoot's History of Mystery class was boring—memorizing silly words and old symbols, and studying ugly plants and magic spells that hadn't worked for centuries, ever since the Great Disempowerment.

But now he really, really wished he had paid more attention in class.

WHY? WHAT
HAPPENED?

Dante tried to remember the right spell.

"   !" he cried.

WHAT SPELL DID
DANTE USE?
DID IT WORK?

STORY #19

WHO ARE
THEY?

KEEP GOING . . .

STORY #19

...CONTINUED

WHAT'S IN THE
BOTTLES?

STORY #19

Emma has always been a scientist.

Her first word was *why*. Ever since, it's been her favorite word—along with *what, how, where, who,* and *when*. All the best words were questions too.

"What," she asked herself one day, "does sand look like up close?" So she got out her microscope and looked . . . and she was gobsmacked! It looked like ....

....

....

....

Emma decided to look at other ordinary things up close. She looked at ....

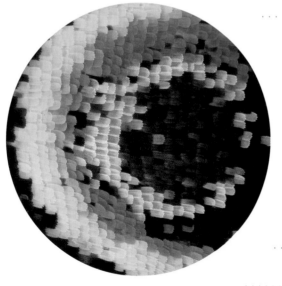

WHAT IS THIS?
HINT: SOMEONE WHO STUDIES OR COLLECTS
THEM IS CALLED A LEPIDOPTERIST!

Next, she decided to look at ....

....

....

And then something crazy

happened ....

....

....

....

WHAT DID SHE
SEE? DRAW IT!

....

....

....

....

....

....

....

....

....

....

....

Zoe is nocturnal. She sleeps all day and is awake all night.

When she was younger, she tried every combination of alarm clocks, hot and cold baths, and warm glasses of milk, but no, she was different and that was just fine. She loved the night time. She loved the quiet, even if it was lonely sometimes.

Tonight, Zoe says good night to her parents and tucks them in, goes to her room and opens the window for some fresh air, and sees a boy. He is sitting wide awake at his desk, drawing by lamplight, in an apartment across the street.

WHO IS THE BOY? WHY IS HE AWAKE?

DO ZOE AND
THE BOY MEET
OR COMMUNICATE?
HOW?

Every second Sunday, Natalie's grandpa came over to play games. Chess, PlayStation, water fights—whatever Natalie liked.

One Sunday, Grandpa arrived and joined Natalie at the kitchen table, where she was waiting with his usual cup of extra strong tea in his favorite mug, the one the size of a fish bowl that said

on the side.

Grandpa sat and sipped. "That might be the best cup of tea I've ever had!" he said, as usual. "How about I choose the game today?"

He pulled a deck of cards from his inside jacket pocket.

Natalie tried not to look disappointed.

"Don't be disappointed," he said. "These are very special cards—magical, actually. Ready?"

He shuffled the deck, faster and faster until his hands were a blur and the cards started to glow orange and gold. The living room lights flickered. The dogs next door howled.

Grandpa stopped and squeezed the deck straight. The lights went back to normal. The dogs became quiet. He put the deck face down on the table.

"Your turn," he said, grinning. "Flip a card."

Natalie looked at him, then the deck, then him, then the deck. She reached out and gently touched the top card—it glowed deeper orange and brighter gold, and felt hot and tingly. She looked at Grandpa. She gulped. She flipped.

STORY #22

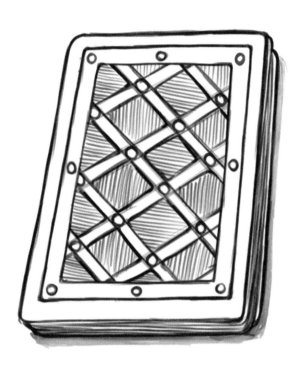

DRAW WHAT WAS ON THE CARD!

WHAT HAPPENED NEXT?

HOW DID THE
GAME END?

STORY #22

Big. Fat. Mistake. and Other Stories We Write Together
Copyright © 2020, 2023 by Rick Benger
All rights reserved.

Published by Collins, an imprint of HarperCollins Publishers Ltd

Previously published in a slightly different form as *Once upon a Pancake for Young Storytellers*
in 2020 by Pfannkuchen Press LLC

First published by Collins in 2023 in this original trade paperback edition

Original illustrations by Matej Beg in story 1; by Maddie Egremont in stories 7, 9, 11, 17, and 21;
by Satria Wahyu in story 8; and by Onofrio Orlando in story 15.
All other images and adapted images are licensed via Shutterstock.

HarperCollins books may be purchased for educational, business,
or sales promotional use through our Special Markets Department.

HarperCollins Publishers Ltd
Bay Adelaide Centre, East Tower
22 Adelaide Street West, 41st Floor
Toronto, Ontario, Canada
M5H 4E3

www.harpercollins.ca

ISBN 978-1-4434-7101-5

Printed and bound in Latvia
PNB 9 8 7 6 5 4 3 2 1

RICK BENGER is the creator of Once upon a Pancake, a series of interactive books with unfinished stories inside. He occasionally writes stories all by himself—a selection of which can be found at rickbenger.com, where you'll also find his newsletter about being a new dad.